THE FULLNESS

A Contemplative Study on the Names of God

Tamara Ramirez

Art by Hannah Fasenmyer

SHAIA-SOPHIA
HOUSE

First Edition

Cover design by Rafael Polendo (polendo.net)
Layout by Tamara Ramirez
Artwork by Hannah Fasenmyer

Unless otherwise identified, all Scripture quotations in this publication are taken from the Holy Bible, New International Version®, NIV®. Copyright ©1973, 1978, 1984, 2011 by Biblica, Inc.™ Used by permission of Zondervan. All rights reserved worldwide. www.zondervan.com The "NIV" and "New International Version" are trademarks registered in the United States Patent and Trademark Office by Biblica, Inc.™

ISBN 978-1-957007-05-2

This volume is printed on acid free paper and meets ANSI Z39.48 standards.

Printed in the United States of America

Published by Shaia-Sophia House
An imprint of Quoir
San Antonio, Texas, USA

www.ShaiaSophiaHouse.com

TABLE OF CONTENTS

"For now we see only a reflection as in a mirror; then we shall see face to face. Now I know in part; then I shall know fully, even as I am fully known."
- 1 Corinthians 13:12

Last year, my sister and I began planning a journey together to visit her friends in Saudi Arabia. We were excited to grow in our understanding of the Muslim faith, deepen our love for Arabic culture, and expand our worldview. Even in our delight, we had to acklowledge our concern about connecting with those we would meet on a spiritual level.

In preparation for our journey, I reached out to a friend who is a Christian pastor with deep love and respect for Muslim people. My hope was to better understand how the Arab, Muslim world views followers of Christ. I also wanted to discover points of spiritual connection. It was in this conversation that the idea for this study first began to come to life.

This friend shared with me a folktale called "The Blind Men and the Elephant." It is most commonly associated with the Persian poet Rumi but has been used as a story to explain the human understanding of God throughout most world religions. The English version of this story is a poem written by American John Godfrey Saxe (see pages 6-7).

I gently held this poem in my heart as our plane landed on Riyadh's desert runway. The moment we walked through the large, glass airport doors and into the warm night, our hearts were opened to the fullness of God that would be revealed to us in Saudi Arabia. Each day I learned something new about The One True God and God's beloved Saudi people. I was struck by the beautiful and faithful rhythms of prayer. A trip to the natural history museum revealed their rootedness in Abraham and respect for Jesus. Conversations with those we met opened my eyes to an aspect of the powerful God they knew, and I had yet to encounter in any meaningful way.

As we traveled, this poem continued to speak to me about how our individual "knowing" of God — whether through scriptural interpretation, personal life experiences, and/or the spiritual encounters of a trusted individual — shape our image of God. I began to wonder how much (or perhaps how little) of the fullness of God I had encountered through my particular life experiences, biblical study, and world view.

This study is a story told, in part, through a foggy glass with great joy and wonder. It is my prayer that it gives us space to contemplate the fullness of God as recorded in scripture — the parts of God we might never have dared touch before. I want to explore the aspects of God offering love and healing, those seemingly harsh or jealous traits which make us feel so uncomfortable that we tend to block them out, and the aspects so wonder-filled that we rarely dare to look at them for fear of losing ourselves.

Over the next few weeks, months, or even years, you are invited to reflect on some of the more common names of God as recorded in scripture. We will contemplate if and how we have seen these aspects of God in our life. Maybe, in the end, we will create a life timeline where we record these God encounters while also identifying the aspects of God we are too scared to meet or have yet to experience.

A Purposeful Cadence

Each chapter highlights a name of God and how I have experienced that name throughout my lifetime. At the end of each chapter, you are invited to spend more time with that aspect of God in three different, but complementary ways.

First, you are given the opportunity to view this name through the eyes of Biblical scholars and Christian writers in the section titled "Deeper Knowing Through the Eyes of Another." This includes references to additional books and podcasts to potentially explore and learn. The authors are varied in their Christian theology. You may disagree with the authors' understanding of scripture but it is my hope that their experiences will invite you into a deeper knowing of God. Consider reading the book in a contemplative manner (slow, self-reflective, and journaled).

You are next welcomed to engage the Biblical text with reflection questions in a section titled "Deeper Discovery Through Sacred Text." Some of you have wounds related to the misuse of scripture. You are encouraged to utilize "The Message" or "Amplified" Bible versions and read with the knowledge that all creation, including you, is fully loved just as it is. If you try and it is still too painful, that is okay. Just skip to the final invitation, "Deeper Connection Through Contemplation."

In the contemplation section of each chapter, you are invited to practice both Lectio and Visio Divina. If you find that you need a few guiding questions in this section, order the discussion guide from TheOverflowLife.Com

Lectio Divina is a Latin phrase that literally translates to "divine reading." It is an ancient contemplative way of praying scripture. This practice invites us to, as St. Benedict says, "listen with the ear of our heart" while holding the desire to encounter God in the center of our being.

The prayer of Visio Divina, or "divine seeing," includes the contemplation of art in prayerful conversation with God. We live in a world constantly inundated with images and Visio Divina requires us to slow down and truly look. With this practice, we open the eyes of our soul, the ears of our heart and see how God is illuminated for us through a piece of beauty. This practice does not require any special knowledge or appreciation of art, just a willingness to attend to and interact with the colors, textures, forms, and overall impressions. It is simply an invitation to wonder.

This study is designed to follow a rhythm and to engage from multiple perspectives, stretching us beyond our norms.

In order to experience this in its fullness, take particular note of the recommended cadence and apply it to each section as we soak in specific traits of God.

Read the Chapter
Meditate on the specific name of God it details.

Sit with the name

Dig deeper

Through the Eyes of Another
references to books/ resources by select Christian scholars and authors

Through Sacred Text
specific scripture passages and questions to consider as we read and ponder them in our heart

Through Contemplation
practicing Visio Divina and Lectio Divina using art/scripture imagery curated specifically for this study and our journey through the names/traits of God

What's In A Name?

Names are powerful. In Judaism, like many other ancient religions, names are believed to reveal an aspect of the person and the depth of the relationship. This is also said to be true of the names of God we will encounter on our journey.

You will notice my difficulty in finding language to adequately honor God's fullness. I chose to use Jehovah instead of YHWH despite the fact it is not found in scripture. I find Jehovah beautifully covered with the fingerprints of humanity. It is a very human attempt to honor and name God. Rooted in Latin, it arose among Christians in the Middle Ages through the combination of the consonants YHWH (JHVH) with the vowels of Adonai ("My Lord"). Though we understand that the name is flawed, it is commonly used today. I find both Jehovah and blind men exploring the parts of an elephant to be great allegories for us, the created, as we explore the fullness of The Divine through God's names.

You may also encounter the growing edges on my use of pronouns in this study. The truth is that God does not fit into a pronoun. For thousands of years, male pronouns were used to identify God; however, in recent years this has been noted to evoke pain. You will see that I have chosen to use all forms of personal pronouns as again, our language is insufficient in the personification of God.

> *"Just as the introduction of God's new name represents a shift in our relationship with God, our different names and titles also symbolize different relationships and interactions."*
>
> - Cantor Martin Levson

Tips For The Journey

- **Go slow.** Take as much time with each aspect of God as you need. It may be days, weeks, or months. Engage in contemplative (gazing at God) practices which include giving God space to speak to our hearts through meditation on scripture, art, and nature. If you want to learn more about Christian contemplation, I suggest the book *"Lectio Divina"* by Christine Painter.

- **Have a journal handy.** When you are sitting with a name of God, write down the thoughts or memories that come to mind, the feelings it evokes, and how your body feels in response. Are you feeling relaxed or are you tense? Taking time to journal brings an experience with God from the head to the heart and offers an invitation to transformation.

- **Get creative.** Find a way to creatively record your encounters with each name of God. It could be a classic timeline recorded on your computer, or a piece of art that captures the beauty of the journey.

- **Gather with others.** Gather a small group of friends and go through the group discussion guide which can be purchased on TheOverflowLife.com. Remember, in spiritual formation small group discussions we practice listening to each experiences and refrain from offering advice or guidance.

- **Continue the journey.** God is infinite and the names in this book are just the beginning. Let this study be the beginning of a lifelong journey of deepening intimacy with the Triune God.

So get your journal, Bible, the Fullness Discussion Guide, concordance, and pens ready. We are about to begin a somewhat near-sighted journey of discovery — a pilgrimage into the fullness of the Triune God.

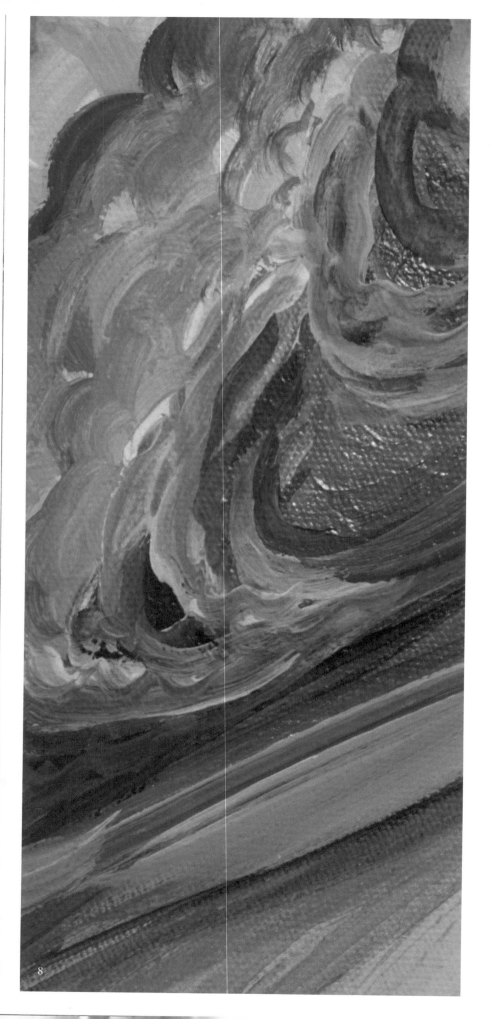

The Blind Men and The Elephant

by American poet John Godfrey Saxe

I.

It was six men of Indostan
To learning much inclined,
Who went to see the Elephant
(Though all of them were blind),
That each by observation
Might satisfy his mind.

II.

The First approached the Elephant,
And happening to fall
Against his broad and sturdy side,
At once began to bawl:
"God bless me!—but the Elephant
Is very like a wall!"

III.

The Second, feeling of the tusk,
Cried: "Ho!—what have we here
So very round and smooth and sharp?
To me 't is mighty clear
This wonder of an Elephant
Is very like a spear!"

IV.

The Third approached the animal,
And happening to take
The squirming trunk within his hands,
Thus boldly up and spake:
"I see," quoth he, "the Elephant
Is very like a snake!"

V.

The Fourth reached out his eager hand,
And felt about the knee.
"What most this wondrous beast is like
Is mighty plain," quoth he;
"'T is clear enough the Elephant
Is very like a tree!"

VI.

The Fifth, who chanced to touch the ear,
Said: "E'en the blindest man
Can tell what this resembles most;
Deny the fact who can,
This marvel of an Elephant
Is very like a fan!"

VII.

The Sixth no sooner had begun
About the beast to grope,
Than, seizing on the swinging tail
That fell within his scope,
"I see," quoth he, "the Elephant
Is very like a rope!"

VIII.

And so these men of Indostan
Disputed loud and long,
Each in his own opinion
Exceeding stiff and strong,
Though each was partly in the right,
And all were in the wrong!

MORAL.

So, oft in theologic wars
The disputants, I ween,
Rail on in utter ignorance
Of what each other mean,
And prate about an Elephant
Not one of them has seen!

INTRODUCTION

The Groom

It was an overcast day in mid-February 1998. It had been raining non-stop for nearly two weeks; but on that day, the clouds parted just enough to offer us a reprieve. The grounds of our Pasadena, California, church were puddled. My faithful friends and family ran around taking care of all the tasks I had forgotten or never thought to do. The church was standing room only — packed full of loved ones and strangers alike. We were running late, but I didn't care. The Ramirez Matriarch had left her home for the first time in 10 years for this event, and we were thrilled. What difference did 45 minutes make?

Then it was time. My 17-year-old brother found me at the back of the church as he took on the role of a father by walking me down the aisle. As the music began and the doors opened into the crowded room, I could see my groom waiting for me. He was 23 years old, a recent college graduate, and a strong, kind man. He stood in his rented tuxedo, surrounded by his closest friends, wearing shoes whose soles bore love notes from his groomsmen.

As I walked toward him, he smiled, and his leg began to twitch with excitement coupled with anxiety. We were young but ready to make a life-long commitment to each other. We had seen beauty in the other and couldn't imagine being without it for the rest of our lives.

I love how God explains His relationship with creation as a marriage. The God-Self representing the Groom and the created, the Bride. We see this as Moses receives the peoples' marriage covenant with "I AM" in the form of two stone tablets (10 commandments) on Mt. Sinai. A golden thread of this commitment of love is wonderfully woven throughout the Psalms, into the Prophets, and then brought to life in the New Testament teachings of Jesus, the gifts of the Spirit, and the first Christian leaders.

As I'm writing this, I also find myself reflecting on my first public commitment to love God with all of my heart, all of my mind, and all of my strength.

I was in the 7th grade and spending a lot of time at a Christian friend's house while my parents wrestled through a messy divorce. I attended church with her on Sunday mornings and participated in the youth group on Wednesday evenings. I was 13, so I was able to join the Presbyterian church's confirmation class where I learned about my Groom and His church. I learned that God was patient, gentle, powerful, and kind. I learned that God loved me, and all I needed to do was love God back. I also walked away with the idea that if I made this commitment to God, then my life would stop being so messy. I soon learned this belief was more troubling than helpful as I journeyed into a deeper relationship with The Divine.

I remember standing in front of the church that day and taking my vow as the pastor lovingly poured water over my head. I remember being so overwhelmed by Love that I began to cry. I recall the church family welcoming me into the community and giving me flowers. That day, much like my wedding day, I knew at a core level I was loved by my Groom and my new family.

What is true about my love relationship with both my husband and the God of the Universe is that on the day I made my vows I only knew one small fragment of their fullness. The years since those commitments have revealed an even bigger tapestry of the beauty in both. I have discovered beauty filled with light and dark, curves and coarseness, intimacy, and unimaginable vastness.

SIDE NOTE: The Bride and Groom metaphor of a love relationship has its limitations. Single individuals or those in same-sex relationships might feel they are excluded from this powerful metaphor. However, this metaphor is intended to communicate an extravagant and unconditional love that develops over a lifetime. This type of love can be found with family members, deep friendships, and in long-term, committed relationships.

REFLECTIONS:

1

JEHOVAH RAAH

Jehovah Rohi; Jehovah Ro'eh; El Ro'i; Yahweh Ro'i; kurios poimainei me
The Lord is my Shepherd

(YEH-HO-VAW' RAW-AW')

Rô'eh from which *Raah* is derived, is commonly translated to "shepherd" in Hebrew. A shepherd is one who feeds or leads their flock to pasture. An extension of the translation of the word rea' is "friend" or "companion." *Jehovah Raah* is the God who is by our side and sees us — even in the darkest places.

I was laying in my grandmother's antique bed safely tucked in under my great-grandmother's homemade quilt. Fear of the next day made it difficult for me to sleep, so I lay in bed listening while the adults watched TV and worked puzzles in grandma's 100-year-old country home. My sister and I spent time every summer in this home. It was the one constant in our childhood. We would fish, take hikes, attend Vacation Bible School, play in her pool, watch TV, and eat all the junk food we could get our hands on. But this year was different.

This was the first summer after my parent's divorce, and, due to mental illness, my dad had become more unpredictable. He was planning to leave the next morning for a week-long backpacking trip. Despite our strained relationship, I was expected to go. I was terrified by the thought of being alone with him. His words had become harsh and demeaning. They robbed me of my dignity and filled me with shame. An encounter with my father left me feeling unworthy of breath. Feeling paralyzed with anxiety, I decided to pray. This was the first time I remember praying for something other than saying thanks for a meal. And, I didn't pray just any prayer, I prayed a very specific prayer. I asked that my Aunt Shelly would convince my father to let me go home with her instead. To my mind, this was a far-fetched idea at best. However, with newfound hope, I drifted off to sleep.

I awoke early as the sunlight was just coming over the White Mountain range and reflecting off the beautiful Sierras. Steeling myself for the week ahead, I walked down the spiral staircase to the smell of breakfast. At the bottom, I was greeted by my aunt. She smiled at me and asked if I wanted to go home with her instead of backpacking. It was at that moment that I felt deeply seen. I knew for the first time that the God of the universe saw me in my pain and heard my cries.

This memory has cradled me during the more messy, challenging, chaotic, and painful times of my life. In truth, some of my heartfelt pleadings have gone seemingly unanswered, but I KNOW God sees me and is guiding me through every valley. She is my Good Shepherd.

Have you experienced the knowing that God sees you?

"I am beginning now to see how radically the character of my spiritual journey will change when I no longer think of God as hiding out and making it as difficult as possible for me to find him, but, instead, as the one who is looking for me while I am doing the hiding."

Henri J.M. Nouwen, "Return of the Prodigal Son"

REFLECTIONS:

SITTING WITH JEHOVAH RAAH

DEEPER KNOWING THROUGH THE EYES OF ANOTHER: *"The Prodigal Son"* by Heni Nouwen

DEEPER DISCOVERY THROUGH SACRED TEXT: Read the stories of Hagar and Ishmael in Genesis 16, Zacchaeus the Tax Collector in Luke 19:1-9, and the story of the prodigal son in Luke 15:11-32. As you read, prayerfully consider times in your life where you felt isolated, alone or afraid. Did you experience a sense of being seen?

DEEPER CONNECTION THROUGH CONTEMPLATION: Spend time in quiet contemplation of the art (*Visio Divina*) and Scripture (*Lectio Divina*) found on pages 14-17.

VISIO DIVINA

• Take 5 minutes of mindful breathing. Take slow deep breaths. This allows your body and mind to become still and open to the movement of the Spirit.

• Look at the image (found on pages 14-17) and let your eyes stay with the very first thing you see. Keep your attention on the one part of the image that first catches your eye. Try to keep your eyes from wandering to other parts of the picture. Breathe deeply and let yourself gaze at that part of the image for a minute or so.

• Let your eyes gaze at the whole image. Take your time and look at every part of the photograph. See it all. Reflect on the image for a minute or so.

• Consider these questions: What emotions does this image evoke in you? What does the image stir up or bring forth in you? Does this image lead you into an attitude of prayer? If so, let these prayers take form in you. Write them down if you desire.

• Take 15 minutes to quietly rest your mind and just be present with God. This type of contemplative prayer does not typically use words.

LECTIO DIVINA

• Take 5 minutes of mindful breathing. Take slow deep breaths. This allows your body and mind to become still and open to the movement of the Spirit.

• Read the Scripture (found on pages 13-16) two times slowly. Listen for a word or phrase that stands out to you and touches your heart. Take a few minutes of silence to breath in that word or phase. Turn it over in your mind and ponder it in your heart.

• Read the Scripture for a third time. Ask God where He is using this word or phrase in your life right now, and take a few minutes in silence.

• Read the Scripture for a final time. Is God inviting you to respond to this Scripture? It may look like action, a new understanding or a creative endeavor.

• Take 15 minutes to quietly rest your mind and just be present with God. This type of contemplative prayer does not typically use words.

JEHOVAH RAAH

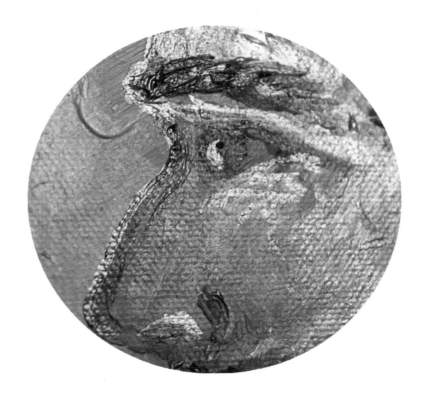

"She gave this name to the Lord who spoke to her: 'You are the God who sees me,' for she said, 'I have now seen the One who sees me'" Genesis 16:13 NIV

REFLECTIONS:

JEHOVAH RAAH

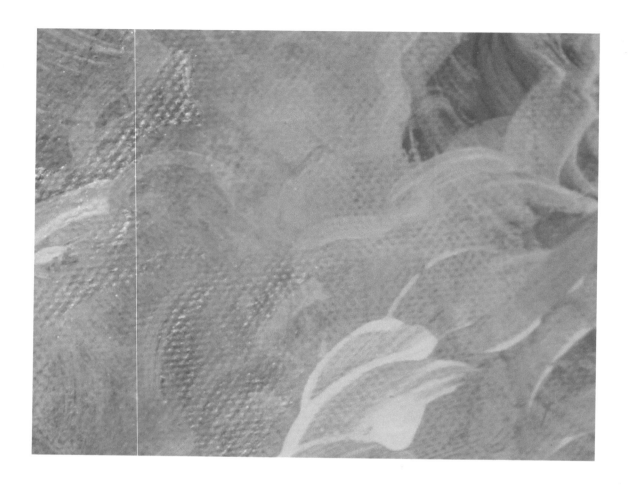

"Hear us, Shepherd of Israel, you who lead Joseph like a flock. You who sit enthroned between the cherubim, shine forth."

Psalm 80:1

REFLECTIONS:

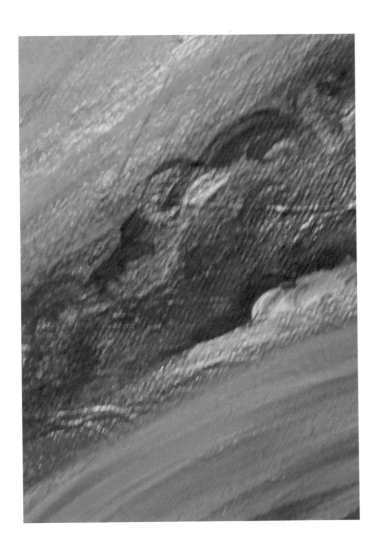

JEHOVAH RAAH

"The Lord is my shepherd; I have everything I need. He lets me rest in fields of green grass and leads me to quiet pools of fresh water."

Psalm 23:1-2

JEHOVAH RAAH

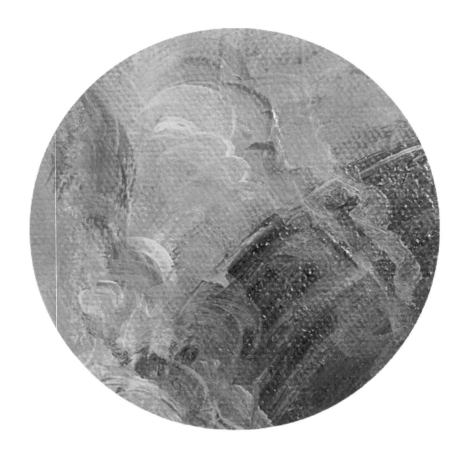

"See, the Sovereign Lord comes with power, and his arm rules for him. See, his reward is with him, and his recompense accompanies him. He tends his flock like a shepherd: He gathers the lambs in his arms and carries them close to his heart; he gently leads those that have young."

Isaiah 40:10-11

REFLECTIONS:

JEHOVAH TSIDKENU

Jehovah Tzidkaynu; Jehovah Tsidqenuw;
kuriou tou theou hêmôn elalêsen pros hêmas
Lord Our Righteousness

(YEH-HO-VAW' TSID-KAY'-NOO)

The name *Jehovah Tsidkenu* draws its meaning from the word tsedek. It translates as rigid or straight. To an Israelite, the word gave a sense of justice and righteousness. As God's people, they were called to walk in integrity on the straight, rigid, and narrow road. In the name *Jehovah Tsidkenu* we are given a picture of our God as one who walks in pure righteousness. As we dig deeper, we come to understand that He is our only source of all that is upright and true.

There are seasons in my life where I can't read whole sections of scripture, specifically the Old Testament. I find I do this when the God I encounter there feels harsh, cruel, and unapproachable. On the surface, Jehovah Tsidkenu makes me want to curl-up into a ball and hide in shame. The idea of a straight, rigid path terrifies me. I find myself feeling like the prophet Isaiah (Isaiah 6) asking God for a lump of hot coal so I can be pure enough to enter the Presence.

Several years ago, I was reading and reflecting on the book of Judges. I was excited and ready: I had my journal labeled, multiple Bible translations, a trusted commentary, and even my multicolored pens. I was ready for God to reveal Himself to me through this book. Tragically, I only made it through the first four chapters before I chose to stop because I did not like the God I encountered. Actually, I felt repulsed and angered by Jehovah Tsidkenu. This God felt harsh, bitter, angry, and bloodthirsty. Yes, the Israelites were unfaithful, disobedient, and living amongst the "wicked," but did so many need to die such cruel deaths? This God appeared to be in opposition to Jesus. I wasn't really sure if I could follow *Jehovah Tsidkenu*. After a three-month break, I picked up the scripture again only to lay it down after 15 more chapters of contemplation. Still today,

I struggle with the paradox of God being both Good Shepherd and the Lord our Righteousness. So what do I do? I hold this aspect of God in tender mystery using the lens of Christ to lovingly gaze on *Jehovah Tsidkenu*. I ask God to reveal *Jehovah Tsidkenu* to me in a way I can understand. I am convinced one day I will get to explore the full beauty found in this aspect of God.

For now, God reminds me that righteousness is
not holding tightly to rules or being perfect
to please a demanding and narrowly focused God.
It is simply to be propelled by love to lay down
self and receive God's gift of righteousness.
As my focus shifts from my inadequacy to God's
abundant love, the straight path opens into a
road as wide as starry skies and as peaceful as a
gentle stream in the valley.

REFLECTIONS:

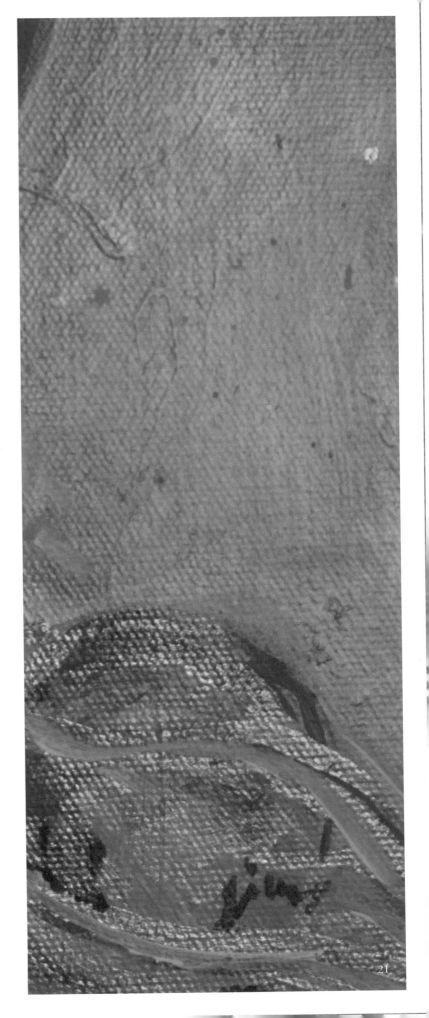

SITTING WITH JEHOVAH TSIDKENU

DEEPER KNOWING THROUGH THE EYES OF ANOTHER: *"The Gifts of the Jews"* by Thomas Cahill; *"What is the Bible"* By Rob Bell (Chapter 8)

DEEPER DISCOVERY THROUGH SACRED TEXT: Read the story of Abraham in Genesis 15:1-6. Note the story of Hagar in chapter 16 in light of this reading. You can also spend time contemplating "The Parable of the Pharisee and the Tax Collector" found in Luke 18. How is God revealing this aspect of The Divine to you?

DEEPER CONNECTION THROUGH CONTEMPLATION: Spend time in quiet contemplation of the art (*Visio Divina*) and Scripture (*Lectio Divina*) found on pages 22-24.

VISIO DIVINA

• Take 5 minutes of mindful breathing. Take slow deep breaths. This allows your body and mind to become still and open to the movement of the Spirit.

• Look at the image (found on pages 22-24) and let your eyes stay with the very first thing you see. Keep your attention on the one part of the image that first catches your eye. Try to keep your eyes from wandering to other parts of the picture. Breathe deeply and let yourself gaze at that part of the image for a minute or so.

• Let your eyes gaze at the whole image. Take your time and look at every part of the photograph. See it all. Reflect on the image for a minute or so.

• Consider these questions: What emotions does this image evoke in you? What does the image stir up or bring forth in you? Does this image lead you into an attitude of prayer? If so, let these prayers take form in you. Write them down if you desire.

• Take 15 minutes to quietly rest your mind and just be present with God. This type of contemplative prayer does not typically use words.

LECTIO DIVINA

• Take 5 minutes of mindful breathing. Take slow deep breaths. This allows your body and mind to become still and open to the movement of the Spirit.

• Read the Scripture (found on pages 20-22) two times slowly. Listen for a word or phrase that stands out to you and touches your heart. Take a few minutes of silence to breath in that word or phrase. Turn it over in your mind and ponder it in your heart.

• Read the Scripture for a third time. Ask God where He is using this word or phrase in your life right now, and take a few minutes in silence.

• Read the Scripture for a final time. Is God inviting you to respond to this Scripture? It may look like action, a new understanding or a creative endeavor.

• Take 15 minutes to quietly rest your mind and just be present with God. This type of contemplative prayer does not typically use words.

REFLECTIONS:

JEHOVAH TSIDKENU

*"In those days Judah will be saved
and Jerusalem will live in safety.
This is the name by which it will
be called: The Lord Our Righteous
Savior"*

Jeremiah 33:16

JEHOVAH TSIDKENU

You see, God's purpose for the law reaches its climax when the Anointed One arrives; now all who trust in Him can have their lives made right with God.

Romans 10:4

JEHOVAH TSIDKENU

"He leadeth me in the paths of righteousness for his name's sake"

Psalm 23:3

REFLECTIONS:

3

JEHOVAH RAPHA

Jehovah-Rophe; Jehovah Rophecha; Jehovah Raphah; kurios ho iômenos se
The Lord That Heals

(YEH-HO-VAW' RAW-FAW')

Rapha means to restore, heal, or make healthful in Hebrew. *Jehovah Rapha* is translated as the God who heals or the Great Physician. We first learn about this aspect of God in Exodus as Moses leads the enslaved Israelites out of Egypt and into the wilderness where they will discover healing, freedom, and restoration through a relationship with God. As we know, this healing did not come instantly or painlessly. Some theologians say it took a week to get the Israelites out of Egyptian slavery and 40 years of wandering in the wilderness to get slavery out of the Israelites and bring about full healing.

We, as the Body of Christ, struggle with Jehovah Rapha. Churches have divided over who, why, and how God heals. We have members of our Christian community who believe that if we are right with God and are full of faith, then He will heal any and all affliction immediately. Others believe God does His healing through human hands or chooses not to heal at all. As a result of our need to claim that we "know" how and why God heals, there is profound pain, feelings of rejection, and division amongst believers.

My friend recently told me about a time when God woke her in the middle of the night to tell her she would soon face an affliction but it would not take her life. Shortly after the night-time message, she was told that she needed to prepare herself and her young family because she had stage IV ovarian cancer. She was informed she would need surgery, chemotherapy, and radiation treatment, but should prepare for death.

As everyone prepared for imminent pain and suffering, she received a call from a friend. This friend explained that God had compelled her to remind my friend of God's promise to not take her life.

"At first I didn't think of it as a gift and begged God to remove it. Three times I did that, and then he told me, "My grace is enough; it's all you need. My strength comes into its own in your weakness." Once I heard that, I was glad to let it happen. I quit focusing on the handicap and began appreciating the gift." 2 Corinthians 12:8-9 MSG

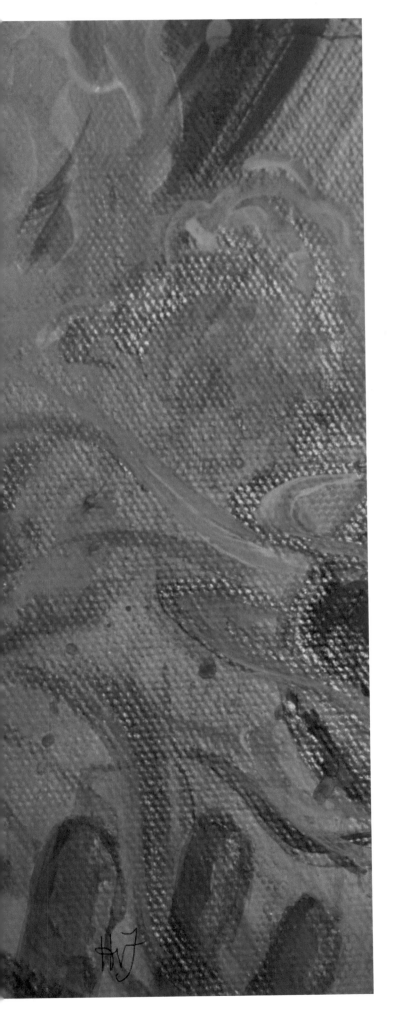

As the surgery approached, the medical team, along with some friends and family, expressed concern that she was in denial and not taking her health seriously enough. Yet still, she sat peacefully in the promise.

The day of the surgery came. She arrived at the prescribed hour and was wheeled into the operating room. A short time later, she was aroused from anesthesia by a smiling surgical team. She was brought to tears when the surgeon told her that, to their surprise, an incision of her abdomen only revealed benign, fluid-filled masses. She was cancer free.

As she healed, all involved began to question if this was a healing miracle or a misdiagnosis? We in the West do this. We want to sort everything into categories: God's healing, medical science, lack of faith, and medical misdiagnosis. I find myself holding tightly to the understanding that God doesn't heal in just one way. Yes, God can heal through tangible miracles. But God can also bring relief through the hands of physicians, gifted counselors, and spiritual directors. God sometimes appears to allow the faithful among us (like the Apostle Paul) to experience prolonged suffering and premature death. I don't know why God doesn't always bring relief from pain. At times, this makes me angry or disillusioned. For now, I hold to the truth that I only see things in part or through a foggy glass. I must let this aspect of God rest in the realm of loving mystery.

I continue to pray for a deeper knowing of Jehovah Rapha.

"We say, then, to anyone who is under trial, give Him time to steep the soul in His eternal truth. Go into the open air, look up into the depths of the sky, or out upon the wideness of the sea, or on the strength of the hills that is His also; or, if bound in the body, go forth in the spirit; spirit is not bound. Give Him time and, as surely as dawn follows night, there will break upon the heart a sense of certainty that cannot be shaken." -Joni Eareckson Tada

REFLECTIONS:

SITTING WITH JEHOVAH RAPHA

DEEPER KNOWING THROUGH THE EYES OF ANOTHER: *"A Place of Healing: Wrestling with the Mysteries of Suffering, Pain, and God's Sovereignty"* by Joni Eareckson Tada; *"Man's Search for Meaning"* by Viktor Frankl; *"Miracles and Other Reasonable Things"* by Sarah Bessey

DEEPER DISCOVERY THROUGH SACRED TEXT: Read about healing in Mark 5 and Jesus' healing of the blind: Jer 3:22; Jer 30:17; Isa 30:26; Isa 61:1; Psa 103:3

Spend time in prayer asking God to sit with you in the tensions we experience with *Jahovah Rapha*.

DEEPER CONNECTION THROUGH CONTEMPLATION: Spend time in quiet contemplation of the art (*Visio Divina*) and Scripture (*Lectio Divina*) found on pages 29-31.

VISIO DIVINA

• Take 5 minutes of mindful breathing. Take slow deep breaths. This allows your body and mind to become still and open to the movement of the Spirit.

• Look at the image (found on pages 29-31) and let your eyes stay with the very first thing you see. Keep your attention on the one part of the image that first catches your eye. Try to keep your eyes from wandering to other parts of the picture. Breathe deeply and let yourself gaze at that part of the image for a minute or so.

• Let your eyes gaze at the whole image. Take your time and look at every part of the photograph. See it all. Reflect on the image for a minute or so.

• Consider these questions: What emotions does this image evoke in you? What does the image stir up or bring forth in you? Does this image lead you into an attitude of prayer? If so, let these prayers take form in you. Write them down if you desire.

• Take 15 minutes to quietly rest your mind and just be present with God. This type of contemplative prayer does not typically use words.

LECTIO DIVINA

• Take 5 minutes of mindful breathing. Take slow deep breaths. This allows your body and mind to become still and open to the movement of the Spirit.

• Read the Scripture (found on pages 27-29) two times slowly. Listen for a word or phrase that stands out to you and touches your heart. Take a few minutes of silence to breath in that word or phase. Turn it over in your mind and ponder it in your heart.

• Read the Scripture for a third time. Ask God where He is using this word or phrase in your life right now, and take a few minutes in silence.

• Read the Scripture for a final time. Is God inviting you to respond to this Scripture? It may look like action, a new understanding or a creative endeavor.

• Take 15 minutes to quietly rest your mind and just be present with God. This type of contemplative prayer does not typically use words.

"He took on our sins in His body when He died on the cross so that we, being dead to sin, can live for righteousness. As the Scripture says, "Through His wounds, you were healed."

1 Peter 2:24

REFLECTIONS:

JEHOVAH RAPHA

"The Lord rebuilds Jerusalem; He gathers Israel's exiled people. He heals the brokenhearted and binds up their wounds."

Psalm 147:2-3

REFLECTIONS:

JEHOVAH RAPHA

"He said, 'If you listen carefully to the Lord your God and do what is right in his eyes, if you pay attention to his commands and keep all his decrees, I will not bring on you any of the diseases I brought on the Egyptians, for I am the Lord, who heals you'"

Exodus 15:26

JEHOVAH MEKODDISHKEM

Jehovah M'kaddesh; kurios ho hagiazôn humas
The Lord our Sanctifier

(YEH-HO-VAW' M-QADASH)

Jehovah Mekoddishkem appears only twice in the scriptures, both after a presentation of the law. It portrays the Lord as our means of sanctification or as the one who sets believers apart for His Glory. The words "sanctify," "holy," and "set apart" all come from the Hebrew word *qâdash*. *Mekoddishkem* originates from this same root word. Therefore, it is commonly understood that the name *Jehovah Mekoddishkem* means "God Who Sets You Apart" or the "God Who Makes You Holy."

As I spend time with *Jehovah Mekoddishkem*, I am reminded of a story told by Henri Nouwen in his book "Life of the Beloved."

Best-selling author Henri Nouwen was a Roman Catholic priest who worked as a seminary professor at both Yale and Harvard. In his later years, he left the academic world behind to serve as chaplain at an organization where severely mentally and physically disabled people live in a community with those of normal abilities. Nouwen and others have found that in

such a place, caregiving moves in both directions, with those in a caregiving role often feeling like they are the ones being cared for. In this story, Henri describes how a disabled community member named Janet came up and asked him for a blessing. He was busy, so he mindlessly traced the sign of the cross on her forehead.

In response, Janet protested, "No, I want a real blessing!"

Realizing her real need, he promised to give her a special blessing at the end of the prayer service. Keeping to his promise, Henri made an announcement at the end of the prayer service, "Janet has asked me for a special blessing."

She walked up to him and wrapped her arms around him. As they held each other, Henri said "Janet, I want you to know that you are God's Beloved Daughter. You are precious in God's eyes. Your beautiful smile, your kindness to the people in your house, and all the good things you do show what a beautiful human being you are. I know you feel a little low these days and that there is some sadness in your heart, but I want you to remember who you are: a very special person, deeply loved by God and all the people who are here with you."

Janet raised her head and looked at him. Her beaming smile told him that she truly understood and received the blessing. Just like Abraham in Genesis 12, the disciples and all of us, she was set apart and blessed. With that sanctified blessing, she became a blessing to others. She ushered in the Kingdom.

Have you been experienced the God that sanctifies and sets you apart to be a blessing?

REFLECTIONS:

SITTING WITH JEHOVAH MEKODDISHKEM

DEEPER KNOWING THROUGH THE EYES OF ANOTHER: *"Life of the Beloved"* by Henri Nouwen

DEEPER DISCOVERY THROUGH SACRED TEXT: Read Luke 5:1-11 (Jesus calls His first disciples), Genesis 12 (The call of Abraham), the book of Esther and/or the book of Jonah. As you read, prayerfully consider how God has set you apart or given you a blessing that overflowed to those around you.

DEEPER CONNECTION THROUGH CONTEMPLATION: Spend time in quiet contemplation of the art (*Visio Divina*) and Scripture (*Lectio Divina*) found on pages 36-37.

VISIO DIVINA

• Take 5 minutes of mindful breathing. Take slow deep breaths. This allows your body and mind to become still and open to the movement of the Spirit.

• Look at the image (found on pages 33-34) and let your eyes stay with the very first thing you see. Keep your attention on the one part of the image that first catches your eye. Try to keep your eyes from wandering to other parts of the picture. Breathe deeply and let yourself gaze at that part of the image for a minute or so.

• Let your eyes gaze at the whole image. Take your time and look at every part of the photograph. See it all. Reflect on the image for a minute or so.

• Consider these questions: What emotions does this image evoke in you? What does the image stir up or bring forth in you? Does this image lead you into an attitude of prayer? If so, let these prayers take form in you. Write them down if you desire.

• Take 15 minutes to quietly rest your mind and just be present with God. This type of contemplative prayer does not typically use words.

LECTIO DIVINA

• Take 5 minutes of mindful breathing. Take slow deep breaths. This allows your body and mind to become still and open to the movement of the Spirit.

• Read the Scripture (found on pages 33-34) two times slowly. Listen for a word or phrase that stands out to you and touches your heart. Take a few minutes of silence to breath in that word or phrase. Turn it over in your mind and ponder it in your heart.

• Read the Scripture for a third time. Ask God where He is using this word or phrase in your life right now, and take a few minutes in silence.

• Read the Scripture for a final time. Is God inviting you to respond to this Scripture? It may look like action, a new understanding or a creative endeavor.

• Take 15 minutes to quietly rest your mind and just be present with God. This type of contemplative prayer does not typically use words.

JEHOVAH MEKODDISHKEM

"God spoke to Moses: 'Tell the Israelites, above all, keep my Sabbaths, the sign between me and you, generation after generation, to keep the knowledge alive that I am the God who makes you holy.'"

Exodus 31:12-13

REFLECTIONS:

REFLECTIONS:

JEHOVAH MEKODDISHKEM

"'The nations will realize that I, God, make Israel holy when my holy place of worship is established at the center of their lives forever.'"

Ezekiel 37:28

5

IMMANU EL

Immanuel; Emmanuel; Immanu El
God With Us

(IH-MAN-YOO-UHL)

"*EL*" is used when talking about God about 200 times in the Bible. It is thought to be the simple form of *Elohim* that is combined with other traits of God to create emphasis. "*Im*" in Hebrew means "with." When these two words are combined, we get "God with us."

Most commonly when we hear the name Immanuel we think of Jesus. We are reminded of God's fulfillment of Isaiah's prophecy. "The virgin shall be with child, and bear a son, and shall name him Immanuel" (Isaiah 7:14). Christian trinitarian doctrine teaches that *Immanu El* has been in existence since the garden. In Genesis we read about the Divine's desire to walk with Adam and Eve in the cool of the evening. However, since that first bite of fruit from the tree of knowledge, God has been pursuing creation and inviting us back into His with-ness. It is near impossible to read any story in both the Old and New Testaments and not see this aspect of the triune God.

As I sit with Immanuel, I have to ask myself do I really believe that with my every breath God is with me?

With that prayerful question comes the reminder of Presence when my father's mental illness led him to divorce my mother, Presence through a very difficult pregnancy, Presence in miscarriages, Presence as I faced impossible decisions, Presence through health complications, and Presence at the near loss of my daughter. The Presence took the form of a friend offering a meal, a kind note, an encouraging word, a held hand, or just a sense of knowing. It was a presence or with-ness that gave me the strength to take my next breath.

"But surrender is only possible if we have total assurance that we are safe. We must be convinced that if we let go we will be caught. This assurance only comes when we trust that our heavenly Father desires to be with us and will not let us fall." - Skye Jethani

REFLECTIONS:

SITTING WITH IMMANU EL

DEEPER KNOWING THROUGH THE EYES OF ANOTHER: "With" by Skye Jethani; "Heart and Mind; The Four-Gospel Journey for Radical Transformation, (3rd.Edition)" by Alexander Shaia

DEEPER DISCOVERY THROUGH SACRED TEXT: Read Joshua 1-6. As you study this era in the life of God's people where do you see Immanuel? Where do you see this aspect of God with you right now and in your darkest moments?

DEEPER CONNECTION THROUGH CONTEMPLATION: Spend time in quiet contemplation of the art (*Visio Divina*) and Scripture (*Lectio Divina*) found on pages 42-43.

VISIO DIVINA

• Take 5 minutes of mindful breathing. Take slow deep breaths. This allows your body and mind to become still and open to the movement of the Spirit.

• Look at the image (found on pages 42-43) and let your eyes stay with the very first thing you see. Keep your attention on the one part of the image that first catches your eye. Try to keep your eyes from wandering to other parts of the picture. Breathe deeply and let yourself gaze at that part of the image for a minute or so.

• Let your eyes gaze at the whole image. Take your time and look at every part of the photograph. See it all. Reflect on the image for a minute or so.

• Consider these questions: What emotions does this image evoke in you? What does the image stir up or bring forth in you? Does this image lead you into an attitude of prayer? If so, let these prayers take form in you. Write them down if you desire.

• Take 15 minutes to quietly rest your mind and just be present with God. This type of contemplative prayer does not typically use words.

LECTIO DIVINA

• Take 5 minutes of mindful breathing. Take slow deep breaths. This allows your body and mind to become still and open to the movement of the Spirit.

• Read the Scripture (found on pages 38-39) two times slowly. Listen for a word or phrase that stands out to you and touches your heart. Take a few minutes of silence to breath in that word or phrase. Turn it over in your mind and ponder it in your heart.

• Read the Scripture for a third time. Ask God where He is using this word or phrase in your life right now, and take a few minutes in silence.

• Read the Scripture for a final time. Is God inviting you to respond to this Scripture? It may look like action, a new understanding or a creative endeavor.

• Take 15 minutes to quietly rest your mind and just be present with God. This type of contemplative prayer does not typically use words.

REFLECTIONS:

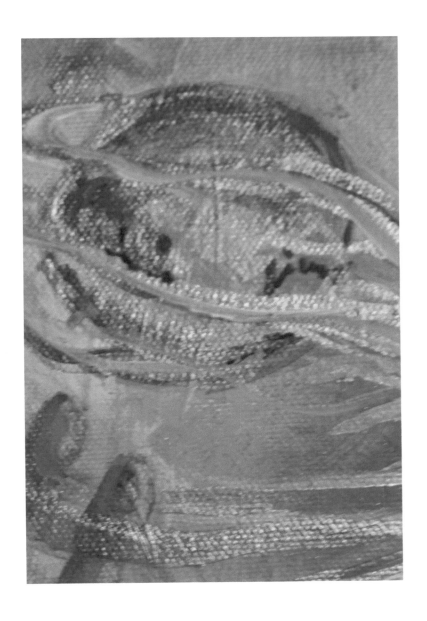

IMMANU EL

"Listen! The virgin shall conceive a child! She shall give birth to a Son, and he shall be called 'Emmanuel' (meaning "God is with us")."

Matthew 1:23

IMMANU EL

"This flood will overflow all its channels and sweep into Judah until it is chin deep. It will spread its wings, submerging your land from one end to the other, O Immanuel."

Isaiah 8: 7b-8

REFLECTIONS:

6

JEHOVAH NISSI

Jehovah Nisi; Jehovahnissi; kurios kataphugê mou
The Lord our Banner

(YEH-HO-VAW' NIS-SEE')

Nes (nês), or *Nissi* means "banner" in Hebrew. In Exd 17:15, Moses defeats the Amalekites and builds an altar named *Jehovah-Nissi* (the Lord our Banner). Nes is sometimes also translated as a pole with a flag type insignia attached. In battle, warring nations would fly their flag on a pole at each of their respective front lines. This gave soldiers a feeling of hope for victory and a focal point. By calling God "our Banner" we are stating that we will keep our eyes on Her alone as our source of hope.

I write this in a year characterized by crashing waves. We find ourselves amid a global pandemic, economic crisis, profound natural disasters, deepening understanding of racism, and an intense presidential election. To say things are tense is an understatement. The body of Christ, which was already experiencing warlike strain over human sexuality, is now even more polarized. Christians are fighting over the wearing of masks, the ideologies of the "Black Lives Matter" movement, and which presidential nominee best represents the Christian worldview. Now, more than ever, we need *Jehovah Nissi*. We need to turn our eyes to The Lord Our Banner of Hope. What would it look like if we, as the followers of "The Way," took our eyes off all that divides us in order to stand and support one another as we seek to keep our eyes on God — Our Banner?

REFLECTIONS:

SITTING WITH JEHOVAH NISSI

DEEPER KNOWING THROUGH THE EYES OF ANOTHER: *"Pray As You Go" app, Sacredpilgrim.org, "When Faith Becomes Sight"* by Beth A. Booram and David Booram

DEEPER DISCOVERY THROUGH SACRED TEXT: Read Exodus 17 and Matthew 14 (focus on Peter walking on water). Where are your eyes focused right now? Are you able to keep your eyes on God while moving into action to care for the "least of these"?

DEEPER CONNECTION THROUGH CONTEMPLATION: Spend time in quiet contemplation of the art (*Visio Divina*) and Scripture (*Lectio Divina*) found on pages 42-43.

VISIO DIVINA

- Take 5 minutes of mindful breathing. Take slow deep breaths. This allows your body and mind to become still and open to the movement of the Spirit.

- Look at the image (found on pages 42-43) and let your eyes stay with the very first thing you see. Keep your attention on the one part of the image that first catches your eye. Try to keep your eyes from wandering to other parts of the picture. Breathe deeply and let yourself gaze at that part of the image for a minute or so.

- Let your eyes gaze at the whole image. Take your time and look at every part of the photograph. See it all. Reflect on the image for a minute or so.

- Consider these questions: What emotions does this image evoke in you? What does the image stir up or bring forth in you? Does this image lead you into an attitude of prayer? If so, let these prayers take form in you. Write them down if you desire.

- Take 15 minutes to quietly rest your mind and just be present with God. This type of contemplative prayer does not typically use words.

LECTIO DIVINA

- Take 5 minutes of mindful breathing. Take slow deep breaths. This allows your body and mind to become still and open to the movement of the Spirit.

- Read the Scripture (found on pages 42-43) two times slowly. Listen for a word or phrase that stands out to you and touches your heart. Take a few minutes of silence to breath in that word or phrase. Turn it over in your mind and ponder it in your heart.

- Read the Scripture for a third time. Ask God where He is using this word or phrase in your life right now, and take a few minutes in silence.

- Read the Scripture for a final time. Is God inviting you to respond to this Scripture? It may look like action, a new understanding or a creative endeavor.

- Take 15 minutes to quietly rest your mind and just be present with God. This type of contemplative prayer does not typically use words.

JEHOVAH-NISSI

"God said to Moses, 'Write this up as a reminder to Joshua, to keep it before him, because I will most certainly wipe the very memory of Amalek off the face of the Earth.' Moses built an altar and named it 'God My Banner.'"

Exodus 17:14-15

REFLECTIONS:

REFLECTIONS:

JEHOVAH-NISSI

"But we thank God for giving us the victory as conquerors through our Lord Jesus, the Anointed One."

1 Corinthians 15:57

JEHOVAH SABAOTH

Elohim Sabaoth; kurios sabaôth
Lord of Hosts or Lord of Powers

(YEH-HO-VAW' SE BA'ÔT)

The Hebrew word *Sabaoth* is commonly translated into English as "hosts" or "armies." In its most literal sense, *Jehovah Sabaoth* reveals God as the commander of the armies reigning over earth, the stars of the universe, and the heavenly realm. Ultimately, all things — both seen and unseen — are under Their royal command.

I am a pacifist by nature. The idea of one man killing another in the name of God is incomprehensible to me. But here it is… God's name… The Lord of Powers, Armies, and Hosts. It conjures images of God pouring out fire on the enemies of Their people much like an angry parent storming the baseball field and attacking the little league pitcher that just beamed their child with the ball. If this is what is meant by Jehovah Sabaoth, then I will only join Them out of self-preservation.

As I sit and ask God to tell me about this aspect of the Godself, I am reminded of a sermon by Rev. C. H. Spurgeon in 1857 on Zechariah 4:6.

"Not by might, nor by power, but by My Spirit, says the Lord of Hosts."

In this sermon he takes his listeners on a journey through each aspect of this verse.

"NOT BY MIGHT, NOR BY POWER.' I answer, yes. The best Hebrew scholars tell us that the, "might," in the first place, may be translated, "army." The Septuagint (Greek version of the Old Testament) does so translate it. It signifies power collectively — the power of a number of men combined together. The second word, "power," signifies the prowess of a single individual, so that I might paraphrase my text thus — "Not by the combined might of men laboring to assist each other, nor by the separate might of any single hero, but by My Spirit, says the Lord."

I only allow myself to approach this terrifying aspect of God when I hit the end of myself or when I start saying things like, "it just is," "we will see," or "there has got to be another way." As a hospice nurse, I have often found myself without communal and individual solutions to my patient's pain. It was in these times I was forced to get out of the way. I would turn to the God of Angel Armies and allow Them to intervene in the way They saw fit.

When do you find yoursef kneeling at the throne of *Jehovah Sabaoth*? What must happen inside of you to get to this place?

"Did we in our own strength confide,
Our striving would be losing;
Were not the right Man on our side,
The Man of God's own choosing;
Dost ask who that may be?
Christ Jesus, it is He;
Lord Sabaoth, His name,
From age to age the same,
And He must win the battle.
A Mighty Fortress is Our God"

"A Mighty Fortress Is Our God"

REFLECTIONS:

SITTING WITH JEHOVAH SABAOTH

DEEPER KNOWING THROUGH THE EYES OF ANOTHER: BibleProject podcast, episode 216-218 on your favorite streaming platform.

DEEPER DISCOVERY THROUGH SACRED TEXT: Spend time prayerfully reading about Mary, Elizabeth, and Zechariah in Luke 1. How is Jehovah Sabaoth revealed to you in this scripture?

DEEPER CONNECTION THROUGH CONTEMPLATION: Spend time in quiet contemplation of the art (*Visio Divina*) and Scripture (*Lectio Divina*) found on pages 52-54.

VISIO DIVINA

•Take 5 minutes of mindful breathing. Take slow deep breaths. This allows your body and mind to become still and open to the movement of the Spirit.

•Look at the image (found on pages 47-49) and let your eyes stay with the very first thing you see. Keep your attention on the one part of the image that first catches your eye. Try to keep your eyes from wandering to other parts of the picture. Breathe deeply and let yourself gaze at that part of the image for a minute or so.

•Let your eyes gaze at the whole image. Take your time and look at every part of the photograph. See it all. Reflect on the image for a minute or so.

•Consider these questions: What emotions does this image evoke in you? What does the image stir up or bring forth in you? Does this image lead you into an attitude of prayer? If so, let these prayers take form in you. Write them down if you desire.

•Take 15 minutes to quietly rest your mind and just be present with God. This type of contemplative prayer does not typically use words.

LECTIO DIVINA

•Take 5 minutes of mindful breathing. Take slow deep breaths. This allows your body and mind to become still and open to the movement of the Spirit.

•Read the Scripture (found on pages 47-49) two times slowly. Listen for a word or phrase that stands out to you and touches your heart. Take a few minutes of silence to breath in that word or phase. Turn it over in your mind and ponder it in your heart.

•Read the Scripture for a third time. Ask God where He is using this word or phrase in your life right now, and take a few minutes in silence.

•Read the Scripture for a final time. Is God inviting you to respond to this Scripture? It may look like action, a new understanding or a creative endeavor.

•Take 15 minutes to quietly rest your mind and just be present with God. This type of contemplative prayer does not typically use words.

JEHOVAH SABAOTH

*"Who is this King-Glory? God, armed and battle-
ready. Wake up, you sleepyhead city! Wake up,
you sleepyhead people! King-Glory is ready to
enter. Who is this King-Glory? God-of-the-Angel-
Armies: He is King-Glory."*

Psalm 24: 8-10

REFLECTIONS:

JEHOVAH SABAOTH

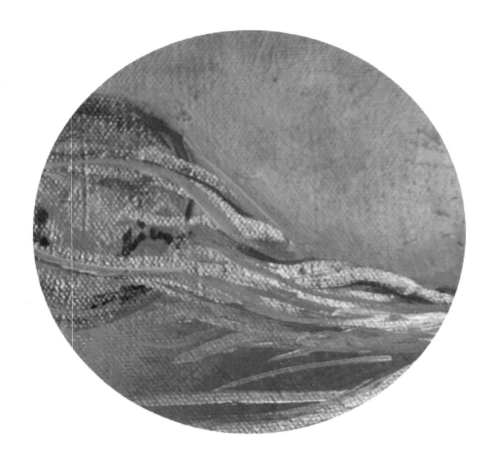

"David answered, "You come at me with sword and spear and battle-ax. I come at you in the name of God-of-the-Angel-Armies, the God of Israel's troops, whom you curse and mock. This very day God is handing you over to me."

1 Samuel 17:45-46

REFLECTIONS:

JEHOVAH SABAOTH

"Therefore the Lord, the Lord Almighty, the Mighty One of Israel, declares: 'Ah! I will vent my wrath on my foes and avenge myself on my enemies."

Isaiah 1:24

8

EL SHADDAI

theou saddai...God Shaddai; pantokratôr (for Shaddai)

The Almighty

(EL SHAD-DI')

There are two different, and on the surface opposing, thoughts regarding the origin and interpretation of the name *El Shaddai*. Translators of the Septuagint (the early Greek translation of Old Testament Hebrew Scriptures) understood the root word of *Shaddai* to be *shadad*, meaning "to overpower." To them, *El Shaddai* pointed toward God's omnipotence and might. Therefore, they translated it to God Almighty. Other translators pointed to the root words of shad meaning "breast" and dai meaning "enough." This would imply that El Shaddai highlights God as a source of nourishment and sufficiency.

As we contemplate the contradiction of these two definitions, they evoke a feeling of a heavenly Mother. The Divine feminine is both all-powerful and intimate provider.

I have a friend who recently told me she was unsure about having kids. When asked why, she said she felt uncertain because she can feel a fierceness rise in her when her dog steps on a thorn and cannot even imagine how she would react if her flesh and blood were in pain. Doesn't she perfectly describe a mother's heart? Mothers are both nurturing and fearfully protective of what we have birthed both physically and spiritually.

REFLECTIONS

SITTING WITH EL SHADDAI

DEEPER KNOWING THROUGH THE EYES OF ANOTHER: *"The Dance of the Dissident Daughter"* by Sue Monk Kidd; *"Eve"* by W.M. Paul Young

DEEPER DISCOVERY THROUGH SACRED TEXT: *Read scripture that speaks of the Sacred Feminine: Hosea 11:3-4 God described as a mother; Isaiah 66:13 God as a comforting mother; Psalm 131:2 God as a mother; Genesis 1:27 Women and men created in God's image.*

DEEPER CONNECTION THROUGH CONTEMPLATION: Spend time in quiet contemplation of the art (*Visio Divina*) and Scripture (*Lectio Divina*) found on pages 57-58.

VISIO DIVINA

• Take 5 minutes of mindful breathing. Take slow deep breaths. This allows your body and mind to become still and open to the movement of the Spirit.

• Look at the image (found on pages 57-58) and let your eyes stay with the very first thing you see. Keep your attention on the one part of the image that first catches your eye. Try to keep your eyes from wandering to other parts of the picture. Breathe deeply and let yourself gaze at that part of the image for a minute or so.

• Let your eyes gaze at the whole image. Take your time and look at every part of the photograph. See it all. Reflect on the image for a minute or so.

• Consider these questions: What emotions does this image evoke in you? What does the image stir up or bring forth in you? Does this image lead you into an attitude of prayer? If so, let these prayers take form in you. Write them down if you desire.

• Take 15 minutes to quietly rest your mind and just be present with God. This type of contemplative prayer does not typically use words.

LECTIO DIVINA

• Take 5 minutes of mindful breathing. Take slow deep breaths. This allows your body and mind to become still and open to the movement of the Spirit.

• Read the Scripture (found on pages 52-53) two times slowly. Listen for a word or phrase that stands out to you and touches your heart. Take a few minutes of silence to breath in that word or phase. Turn it over in your mind and ponder it in your heart.

• Read the Scripture for a third time. Ask God where He is using this word or phrase in your life right now, and take a few minutes in silence.

• Read the Scripture for a final time. Is God inviting you to respond to this Scripture? It may look like action, a new understanding or a creative endeavor.

• Take 15 minutes to quietly rest your mind and just be present with God. This type of contemplative prayer does not typically use words.

REFLECTIONS:

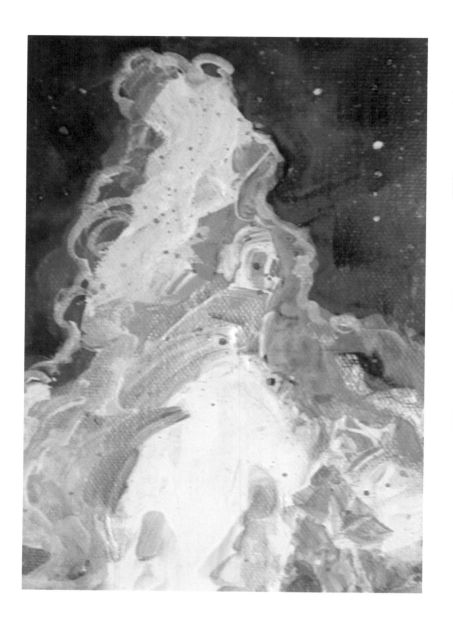

EL SHADDAI

And God said to him, "I am God Almighty; be fruitful and increase in number. A nation and a community of nations will come from you, and kings will be among your descendants.

Genesis 35:11

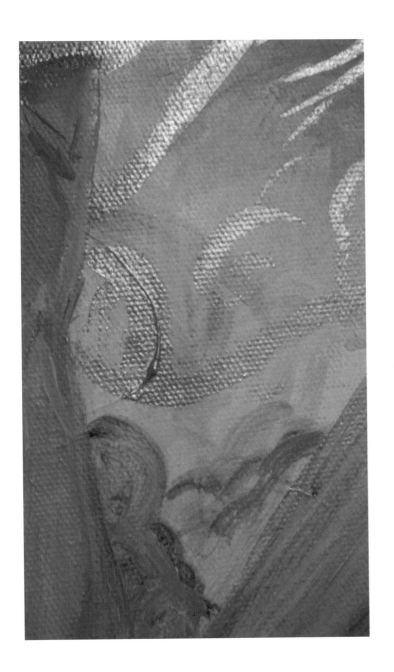

EL SHADDAI

*The Lord thundered from heaven;
the voice of the Most High
resounded.*

Psalm 91:1

9

EL ELYON

ho theos ho hupsistos
God Most High

(EL EL-YONE')

Elyon is found in the Old Testament 28 times and literally means "peak" or uppermost part of a structure or hill. It is most commonly translated in scripture as "Most High" or "the most exalted God." When used, it expresses the extreme sovereignty and majesty of God and His highest preeminence. We first see this name for God in Genesis 14 when Abram encounters Melchizedek.

"Melchizedek, king of Salem, brought out bread and wine — he was a priest of the High God — and blessed him: Blessed be Abram by The High God, Creator of Heaven and Earth. And blessed be The High God, who handed your enemies over to you."

As I consider this aspect of the Divine, I find that it is just as vital for me today as it was for Abram. When Abram and his barren wife Sarai first encountered *El Elyon* in Genesis 12, they worshiped the many gods of Ur. It is in this chapter where God invites Abram to leave all that he knows to follow Him with the promise to make the childless Abram and Sarai into a great nation. As we follow their journey throughout scripture, we see Abram falling asleep to this truth and relying on his own strength, knowledge, and trickery to survive. We see over and over how he thinks he knows better than God when he lies to kings and says Sarai is his sister, saves Lot and his family, and has a child with Hagar. Each time he does this, we see a trail of destruction and pain. Like me, Abram must be reminded repeatedly that there is only one *El Elyon*, and it's not him (or me). We worship a God who is higher than anything made of dust or spirit.

REFLECTIONS:

SITTING WITH EL ELYON

EPER KNOWING THROUGH THE EYES OF ANOTHER: *"How God Became King"* by
N.T. Wright

DEEPER DISCOVERY THROUGH SACRED TEXT: *Read* Matthew 17:1-13; Exodus
24; Psalm 91. Spend some time prayerfull considering how your life
expresses a relationship with El Elyon.

DEEPER CONNECTION THROUGH CONTEMPLATION: Spend time in quiet
contemplation of the art (*Visio Divina*) and Scripture (*Lectio Divina*)
found on pages 61-63.

VISIO DIVINA

• Take 5 minutes of mindful breathing.
Take slow deep breaths. This allows your
body and mind to become still and open
to the movement of the Spirit.

• Look at the image (found on pages 61-
63) and let your eyes stay with the very
first thing you see. Keep your attention
on the one part of the image that first
catches your eye. Try to keep your eyes
from wandering to other parts of the
picture. Breathe deeply and let yourself
gaze at that part of the image for a
minute or so.

• Let your eyes gaze at the whole image.
Take your time and look at every part
of the photograph. See it all. Reflect on
the image for a minute or so.

• Consider these questions: What emotions
does this image evoke in you? What does
the image stir up or bring forth in
you? Does this image lead you into an
attitude of prayer? If so, let these
prayers take form in you. Write them
down if you desire.

• Take 15 minutes to quietly rest your
mind and just be present with God. This
type of contemplative prayer does not
typically use words.

LECTIO DIVINA

• Take 5 minutes of mindful breathing.
Take slow deep breaths. This allows your
body and mind to become still and open
to the movement of the Spirit.

• Read the Scripture (found on pages 56-
58) two times slowly. Listen for a word
or phrase that stands out to you and
touches your heart. Take a few minutes
of silence to breath in that word or
phase. Turn it over in your mind and
ponder it in your heart.

• Read the Scripture for a third time.
Ask God where He is using this word or
phrase in your life right now, and take
a few minutes in silence.

• Read the Scripture for a final time. Is
God inviting you to respond to this
Scripture? It may look like action,
a new understanding or a creative
endeavor.

• Take 15 minutes to quietly rest your
mind and just be present with God. This
type of contemplative prayer does not
typically use words.

EL ELYON

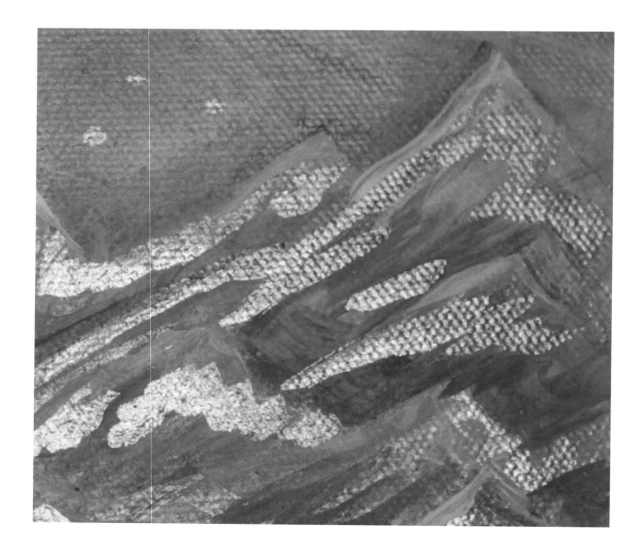

"If you listen obediently to the Voice of God, your God, and heartily obey all his commandments that I command you today, God, your God, will place you on high, high above all the nations of the world"

Deuteronomy 28:1

REFLECTIONS:

REFLECTIONS:

EL ELYON

"The Lord thundered from heaven; the voice of the Most High resounded."

2 Samuel 22:14

EL ELYON

Be good to me, God—and now! I've run to you for dear life. I'm hiding out under your wings until the hurricane blows over. I call out to High God, the God who holds me together. He sends orders from heaven and saves me, he humiliates those who kick me around. God delivers generous love, he makes good on his word.

Psalm 57:2-3

REFLECTIONS:

10

EL OLAM

[ho] theos [ho] aiônios
Eternal God

(EL O-LAWM')

Olam derives from the root word "lm" which means "forever," "eternity," or "everlasting." When the two words are combined with *El*, *El Olam* can be translated as "Eternal God," "Everlasting God," "God of the Universe," or "Ancient of Days." We first hear this name for God in Genesis 21. In this section, Sarah (Sarai) has given birth to Isaac and sent Hagar with Ishamel to survive in the wilderness on their own. Then the always peace-loving and pain-avoiding Abraham (Abram) makes a covenant with the king of the Philistines. To mark this moment, Abraham plants a tamarisk tree to honor *El Olam*.

The tamarisk tree is what we call a salt cedar or athel pine. It is a desert plant and the only tree that can grow around the dead sea. It has a deep root system and possesses the unique ability to bring cooling shade and protection to all who hide in its shadow from inhospitable environments. It does this through tiny gray-green needles that excrete salt on their surfaces. At night water vapor adheres to these salt particles to form droplets. In the morning these tiny droplets of water evaporate and cool the tree and the shade below it.

Many scholars believe Abraham planted this tree to stand as a monument to *El Olam*, or Ancient of Days, for Their descendants. Abraham wanted future generations to remember God went before them and will continue to stand and offer shade and refreshment until their bodies return to the dust.

There is comfort and a feeling of rootedness for me in the shadow of *El Olam*. It reminds me of God's provision enveloping and protecting me even when I, like Abraham, fall short of being all God has asked me to be. I find *El Olam* to be particularly comforting in this era where the culture feels inhospitable for those seeking to walk in the footsteps of Christ.

REFLECTIONS:

SITTING WITH EL OLAM

DEEPER KNOWING THROUGH THE EYES OF ANOTHER: "Intimacy with God" By Thomas Keating

DEEPER DISCOVERY THROUGH SACRED TEXT: Read Psalm 139. Spend time with The Eternal God. Can you feel The Presence around you, through you, and inside of you? If so. is it a feeling of love, protection, care, or something different?

DEEPER CONNECTION THROUGH CONTEMPLATION: Spend time in quiet contemplation of the art (*Visio Divina*) and Scripture (*Lectio Divina*) found on pages 68-69.

VISIO DIVINA

•Take 5 minutes of mindful breathing. Take slow deep breaths. This allows your body and mind to become still and open to the movement of the Spirit.

•Look at the image (found on pages 68-69) and let your eyes stay with the very first thing you see. Keep your attention on the one part of the image that first catches your eye. Try to keep your eyes from wandering to other parts of the picture. Breathe deeply and let yourself gaze at that part of the image for a minute or so.

•Let your eyes gaze at the whole image. Take your time and look at every part of the photograph. See it all. Reflect on the image for a minute or so.

•Consider these questions: What emotions does this image evoke in you? What does the image stir up or bring forth in you? Does this image lead you into an attitude of prayer? If so, let these prayers take form in you. Write them down if you desire.

•Take 15 minutes to quietly rest your mind and just be present with God. This type of contemplative prayer does not typically use words.

LECTIO DIVINA

•Take 5 minutes of mindful breathing. Take slow deep breaths. This allows your body and mind to become still and open to the movement of the Spirit.

•Read the Scripture (found on pages 62-63) two times slowly. Listen for a word or phrase that stands out to you and touches your heart. Take a few minutes of silence to breath in that word or phase. Turn it over in your mind and ponder it in your heart.

•Read the Scripture for a third time. Ask God where He is using this word or phrase in your life right now, and take a few minutes in silence.

•Read the Scripture for a final time. Is God inviting you to respond to this Scripture? It may look like action, a new understanding or a creative endeavor.

•Take 15 minutes to quietly rest your mind and just be present with God. This type of contemplative prayer does not typically use words.

EL OLAM

"But you, Lord, are the true God, you are the living God and the eternal king. When you are angry, the world trembles; the nations cannot endure your anger"

Jeremiah 10:10

REFLECTIONS:

REFLECTIONS:

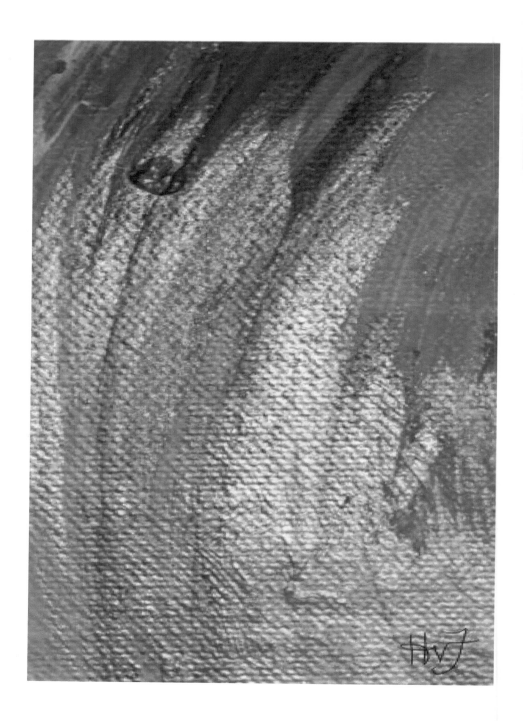

EL OLAM

"Trust in the Lord forever. The Lord himself is the Rock. The Lord will keep us safe forever."

Isaiah 26:4

A Fuller View

In this section of our study, we will
begin to pan out into a fuller vision
of The Triune God. What we have seen,
felt, and experienced will begin to take
a fuller shape, though we hold to the
knowledge that our earthly lens is still
foggy and limited.

As you move forward in the study, take
note of how the images in the first ten
sections become part of a bigger picture.

When you complete chapter 12 consider
reflecting on the previous sections. Are
you able to note where each name fits into
the bigger picture? Where do you still
need to spend time exploring?

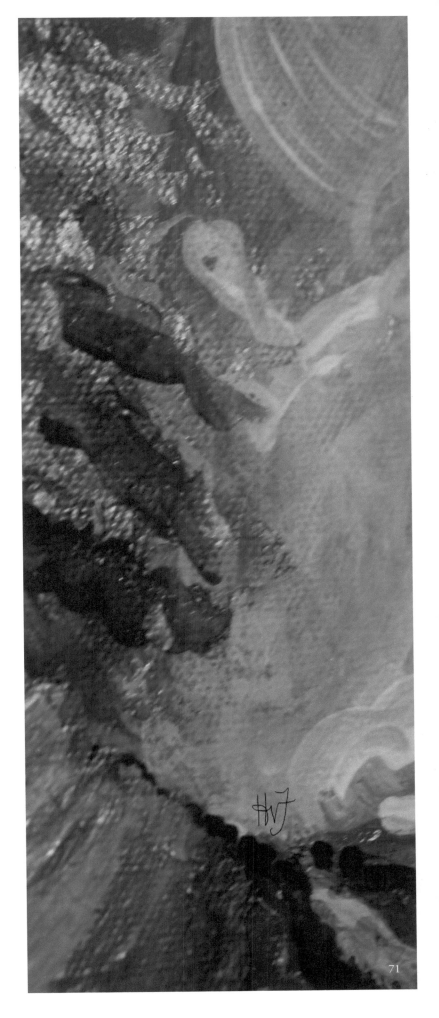

ELOHIM

Elohay; El; theos (the standard Greek word for god); ***Elah; Elo'ah***
God of Gods or God of Fullness to non-Israelites

(EL-O-HEEM')

Elohim is understood to mean God, judge, or creator. It is the first name used for God in the Bible and found more than 2,300 times. *Elohim* is rooted in the Hebrew word for "strength" or "power" and has the characteristic of being plural in form. In Genesis 1:1, we read, "In the beginning, Elohim created the heavens and the earth," and discover this plurality. A plurality the Christian church identifies as the triune mystery of God.

On January 1, 1993, I turned 18 years old and officially declared myself to be an adult. I received several precious gifts that year, but my favorite was a leather-bound NIV Life Application Study Bible. I remember prying open the beautifully designed cardboard box and carefully removing it. I was in awe of this huge book. Its thin, gold-trimmed pages and leathery, new book smell enthralled me.

I spent hours running my fingers over its pages and breathing in the earthy aroma.

After being introduced to God and being baptized in middle school, I became actively engaged in local youth groups, followed Christian principles (as best a teen can), and prayed a bit. So when I got that Bible, I decided it was time for me to actually read the words printed on the page. I decided to start with the New Testament book of Matthew. I loved it so much that I decided to read the next book, Mark, to find out what happens next. To my surprise, the stories were almost the same. Not much for asking questions, I went on to read the books of Luke and John only to find the same thing. I finally mustered the courage and asked a youth pastor why the first four books of the New Testament just repeated the same stories in different ways. Thankfully, he knew the answer and helped me engage in the many mysteries of the Bible for the first time.

Today, I experience the scriptures as a living breathing text. The Bible's pages are encapsulated with wonder-filled mysteries and beautiful invitations to get to know the Triune God. I love how *Elohim* is the first name for God we are introduced to in the Bible. I believe that on the day of my baptism I was introduced *to Elohim* — God of beginnings, creation, and judgement — and fell in love. Over the years, I have come to know God through other names and experienced a deeper knowing, profound love, and unceasing presence.

REFLECTIONS:

SITTING WITH ELOHIM

DEEPER KNOWING THROUGH THE EYES OF ANOTHER: "*Fearfully and Wonderfully: The Marvel of Bearing God's Image*" by Dr. Paul Brand and Phillip Yancey

DEEPER DISCOVERY THROUGH SACRED TEXT: Read and spend time with the aspect of God found in both creation stories (Genesis 1 and Genesis 2). What is your encounter like?

DEEPER CONNECTION THROUGH CONTEMPLATION: Spend time in quiet contemplation of the art (*Visio Divina*) and Scripture (*Lectio Divina*) found on page 74.

VISIO DIVINA

•Take 5 minutes of mindful breathing. Take slow deep breaths. This allows your body and mind to become still and open to the movement of the Spirit.

•Look at the image (found on page 74) and let your eyes stay with the very first thing you see. Keep your attention on the one part of the image that first catches your eye. Try to keep your eyes from wandering to other parts of the picture. Breathe deeply and let yourself gaze at that part of the image for a minute or so.

•Let your eyes gaze at the whole image. Take your time and look at every part of the photograph. See it all. Reflect on the image for a minute or so.

•Consider these questions: What emotions does this image evoke in you? What does the image stir up or bring forth in you? Does this image lead you into an attitude of prayer? If so, let these prayers take form in you. Write them down if you desire.

•Take 15 minutes to quietly rest your mind and just be present with God. This type of contemplative prayer does not typically use words.

LECTIO DIVINA

•Take 5 minutes of mindful breathing. Take slow deep breaths. This allows your body and mind to become still and open to the movement of the Spirit.

•Read the Scripture (found on page 68) two times slowly. Listen for a word or phrase that stands out to you and touches your heart. Take a few minutes of silence to breath in that word or phase. Turn it over in your mind and ponder it in your heart.

•Read the Scripture for a third time. Ask God where He is using this word or phrase in your life right now, and take a few minutes in silence.

•Read the Scripture for a final time. Is God inviting you to respond to this Scripture? It may look like action, a new understanding or a creative endeavor.

•Take 15 minutes to quietly rest your mind and just be present with God. This type of contemplative prayer does not typically use words.

ELOHIM

"In the beginning, God (prepared, formed, fashioned, and) created the heavens and the earth.Peace."

Genesis 1:1 AMPC

ADONAI

Kurios; Adon (Singular Form)
Lord; Master; Majesty (Plural Form)

(AD-O-NOY')

Like *Elohim, Adonai* is a plural of majesty. It is frequently translated in scripture as Lord or Master. When the singular *adon* is used, it usually refers to a human lord. First found in Genesis 15, it is used more than 400 times in the Bible. It is the verbal parallel to *Yahweh and Jehovah*. Many devout in the Jewish faith will use *Adonai* in place of *Yahweh* to ensure that the 7th commandment (do not take the Lord's name in vain) is not inadvertently broken.

I most commonly experience this trait of God in times of deep loss or need. I specifically remember a time when I felt isolated, alone, and surrounded by crashing waves of confusion. It was at my lowest moment when Jesus' recalled words resonated in my mind, "My God, My God, why have you forsaken me." Like Jesus and Job, I both knew and believed God even in the chaos. Nonetheless, I felt pressed on all sides by the weight of our reality. I begged God to bring Their presence and heal my daughter and our family. Yet here I was continuing to cry out until I heard *Adonai* ask me, "Who do you say I AM?" To which my only answer could be… You are Lord, You are Master, You are King.

This understanding of *Adonai* pulls me out

from a fetal position into a standing stance of praise, even in womb-like darkness. I just have to be still and know.

REFLECTIONS:

SITTING WITH ADONAI

DEEPER KNOWING THROUGH THE EYES OF ANOTHER: BibleProject podcast, episode 19-21 on your favorite streaming platform.

DEEPER DISCOVERY THROUGH SACRED TEXT: Read the Book of Job Spend time with God and reflect on what your actions reveal about who you say God is. *Interesting facts, Job is believed to be the first recorded book of the Bible. So could the first question recorded in the Bible be: "My God... why does life hurt so much?"*

DEEPER CONNECTION THROUGH CONTEMPLATION: Spend time in quiet contemplation of the art (*Visio Divina*) and Scripture (*Lectio Divina*) found on page 77.

VISIO DIVINA

• Take 5 minutes of mindful breathing. Take slow deep breaths. This allows your body and mind to become still and open to the movement of the Spirit.

• Look at the image (found on page 77) and let your eyes stay with the very first thing you see. Keep your attention on the one part of the image that first catches your eye. Try to keep your eyes from wandering to other parts of the picture. Breathe deeply and let yourself gaze at that part of the image for a minute or so.

• Let your eyes gaze at the whole image. Take your time and look at every part of the photograph. See it all. Reflect on the image for a minute or so.

• Consider these questions: What emotions does this image evoke in you? What does the image stir up or bring forth in you? Does this image lead you into an attitude of prayer? If so, let these prayers take form in you. Write them down if you desire.

• Take 15 minutes to quietly rest your mind and just be present with God. This type of contemplative prayer does not typically use words.

LECTIO DIVINA

• Take 5 minutes of mindful breathing. Take slow deep breaths. This allows your body and mind to become still and open to the movement of the Spirit.

• Read the Scripture (found on page 71) two times slowly. Listen for a word or phrase that stands out to you and touches your heart. Take a few minutes of silence to breath in that word or phase. Turn it over in your mind and ponder it in your heart.

• Read the Scripture for a third time. Ask God where He is using this word or phrase in your life right now, and take a few minutes in silence.

• Read the Scripture for a final time. Is God inviting you to respond to this Scripture? It may look like action, a new understanding or a creative endeavor.

• Take 15 minutes to quietly rest your mind and just be present with God. This type of contemplative prayer does not typically use words.

"For everything, absolutely everything, above and below, visible and invisible, rank after rank after rank of angels—everything got started in him and finds its purpose in him. He was there before any of it came into existence and holds it all together right up to this moment."

Colossians 1:16-17

REFLECTIONS:

YHWH

Yahweh or Jehovah
I AM

(YOD, HE, VAY, HE)

"YHWH" is the Hebrew word that translates as "LORD." It is used more frequently in the Old Testament than any other name for God. It is a "Tetragrammaton," which means "the four letters." YHVH is derived from the Hebrew verb "to be" and is the special name that God revealed to Moses at the burning bush.

"And God said to Moses, 'I AM WHO I AM; My eternal name, and this is how I am to be recalled for all generations'" (Exodus 3:14-15).

Although some pronounce YHVH as *"Jehovah"* or *"Yahweh,"* scholars really don't know the proper pronunciation. Jewish people stopped pronouncing this name by about 200 AD out of fear of breaking the commandment.

Many Biblical scholars are convinced that the correct pronunciation of *Yahweh* is

an attempt to replicate and imitate the very sound of inhalation and exhalation. Therefore, the one thing we do every moment of our lives is to speak the name of God. This makes the name of God our first and last word as we enter and leave the world.

It's incredibly appropriate that we end this portion of our journey with *YHWH*. Where all the other names were descriptions of God, this is the name God declared for Themself. In the name of *YHVH*, God declares Their absolute fullness of being — eternally of all, in all, and through all.

Can you feel it? The vastness and wonder of the God of the universe entering the depths of you and all around you with every breath? I find this reality to be both profoundly overwhelming and intimately comforting at the same time.

REFLECTIONS

SITTING WITH YHWH

DEEPER KNOWING THROUGH THE EYES OF ANOTHER: *"The Divine Dance"* by Richard Rohr; *"Delighting in the Trinity"* by Michael Reeves

EEPER DISCOVERY THROUGH SACRED TEXT: Read Exodus 3:13-15; Psalm 19 (notice the shift from Elohim to Yahweh). Does it feel like opening or closing? Spend time with Yahweh. Are there spaces in the fullness of the Divine you still want to explore?

DEEPER CONNECTION THROUGH CONTEMPLATION: Spend time in quiet contemplation of the art (*Visio Divina*) and Scripture (*Lectio Divina*) found on page 81.

VISIO DIVINA

• Take 5 minutes of mindful breathing. Take slow deep breaths. This allows your body and mind to become still and open to the movement of the Spirit.

• Look at the image (found on page 81) and let your eyes stay with the very first thing you see. Keep your attention on the one part of the image that first catches your eye. Try to keep your eyes from wandering to other parts of the picture. Breathe deeply and let yourself gaze at that part of the image for a minute or so.

• Let your eyes gaze at the whole image. Take your time and look at every part of the photograph. See it all. Reflect on the image for a minute or so.

• Consider these questions: What emotions does this image evoke in you? What does the image stir up or bring forth in you? Does this image lead you into an attitude of prayer? If so, let these prayers take form in you. Write them down if you desire.

• Take 15 minutes to quietly rest your mind and just be present with God. This type of contemplative prayer does not typically use words.

LECTIO DIVINA

• Take 5 minutes of mindful breathing. Take slow deep breaths. This allows your body and mind to become still and open to the movement of the Spirit.

• Read the Scripture (found on page 74) two times slowly. Listen for a word or phrase that stands out to you and touches your heart. Take a few minutes of silence to breath in that word or phrase. Turn it over in your mind and ponder it in your heart.

• Read the Scripture for a third time. Ask God where He is using this word or phrase in your life right now, and take a few minutes in silence.

• Read the Scripture for a final time. Is God inviting you to respond to this Scripture? It may look like action, a new understanding or a creative endeavor.

• Take 15 minutes to quietly rest your mind and just be present with God. This type of contemplative prayer does not typically use words.

"Tell the I AM"

Exodus 3:14 interpetation

REFLECTIONS:

FINAL THOUGHTS

Then, by constantly using your faith, the life of Christ will be released deep inside you, and the resting place of his love will become the very source and root of your life. Then you will be empowered to discover what every holy one experiences—the great magnitude of the astonishing love of Christ in all its dimensions. How deeply intimate and far-reaching is his love! How enduring and inclusive it is! Endless love beyond measurement that transcends our understanding—this extravagant love pours into you until you are filled to overflowing with the fullness of God!

- Ephesians 3:17-19

May Paul's writings to the Espesians become our prayer:

"Lord I come before you desiring to know, feel and be transformed by the fullness of YOU. May I feel your strong, loving comfort as I lay down all of who I am to simply gaze on your great, powerful, terrifying glory." Amen.

If you would like to continue on this journey of discovery consider using the resources given on the next page to engage in some of the other names of GOD.

- JEHOVAH-SHAMMAH
- SHAPHAT
- EL-BERITH
- GAOL
- EYALUTH
- EL-GIBHOR
- MAGEN
- KANNA
- JEHOVAH-SHALOM

Hannah Fasenmyer

Hannah has been drawing and painting since before she can remember. She majored in art for one year at Texas A&M University before switching to education. She currently lives in San Antonio, Texas with her husband Jeremy where they both teach at a classical public charter school. Teaching and art are two passions she holds dear and she is thankful for the opportunity to currently be pursuing them both.

INSPIRATION FOR THIS PIECE

There is this moment, this intake of breath, before God speaks the world into being. After this intake of breath, there is an explosion of sound, light, color, matter, texture, and life. This moment when God speaks the world into being is not one of chaos. It is life in its purest, rawest form.

I do not know the actual happenings of the mystery of that moment when God breathed life into the still quiet frame of the universe. But it is the mystery and wonder of this moment, this birth of life itself, that inspires many of my paintings. When I paint, I think I am trying to be with God, trying to be with Him in that moment of creation. I want to take part in His breathing and speaking.

He has put a peculiar sort of breath inside of me, the kind of breath that doesn't just give my frame life, but wants to go on producing life within other frames.

RESOURCES

Websites

bible.org

allaboutgod.com

hebrew4christians.com

blueletterbible.org

lwf.org

christianity.com

jesusfilm.org

allaboutjesuschrist.org

loyolapress.com/catholic-resources

hebrew-streams.org

Sacredpilgrim.com

Apps

Pray As You Go

Headspace

Centering Prayer

Podcasts

BibleProject

Books

"What is the Bible? How an Ancient Library of Poems, Letters, and Stories Can Transform the Way You Think and Feel About Everything"
By Rob Bell

"Miracles and Other Reasonable Things" by Sarah Bessey

"When Faith Becomes Sight"
Beth A. Booram and David Booram

"Fearfully and Wonderfully: The Marvel of Bearing God's Image"
Dr. Paul Brand and Phillip Yancey

"The Gifts of the Jews"
Thomas Cahill

"A Place of Healing" Joni Eareckson Tada

"Man's Search for Meaning"
Viktor Frankl

"With: Reimagining the Way You Relate to God"
Skye Jethani

"Intimacy with God"
Thomas Keating

"The Dance of the Dissident Daughter"
Sue Monk Kidd

"Return of the Prodigal Son" &
"Life of the Beloved"
Henri J.M. Nouwen

"Delighting in the Trinity"
Michael Reeves

"The Divine Dance"
Richard Rohr

The Four-Gospel Journey for Radical Transformation,(3rd.Edition)
Alexander Shaia

"How God Became King"
N.T. Wright

"Eve"
William Paul Young